W9-COT-011

I Am How I Pray

The Little Book for Praying Like Jesus

Dr. Shane Stanford

A Journey Points with Jesus **Series**

Jericho Springs Press

Memphis, TN

This is a publication of Jericho Springs Press in Memphis, TN.

A scripture references are from the Common English Bible
Translation from Abingdon Press.

ISBN:10:-0692403027
ISBN-13:9780692403020

DEDICATION

For Christ's Church at Christ Church.

Be Salt and Light… You Matter!

CONTENTS

ACKNOWLEDGMENTS

As with every book or project that I have written, it is impossible to say 'thank you' to every one who has played a part in making this process successful. I am very blessed with numerous friends and colleagues, along with a wonderful congregation that allows me the opportunity to share my heart and the Good News of Jesus Christ through the written word. So, 'thank you' to all of you who stand in the gap for me each and every time.

However, there are a few special individuals who not only make what I do worth it, but they make each day mean something deep and personal for my life. Without you guys, I am nothing. I love you all.

To my staff and friends at Christ Church, Memphis and Christ Church Global. To Dr. Maxie Dunnam, who is more than a mentor but a dear friend whose wisdom has changed my life. To my parents, sister, and in-laws whose constant support and confidence allow me courage to act boldly over the horizon. And, to my girls—all four of them- Pokey, Sarai Grace, Juli Anna and Emma Leigh— for being my inspiration and the real reason why I want to make sure what I am saying to God means something more than my feeble, simple mind can know or understand. I love you guys.

Shane Stanford

AN OPENING WORD

Dear Friend,

Journey Points with Jesus is a resource series developed and published by Jericho Springs Press and Christ Church Global (CCG). CCG is the resource and media outreach division of Christ Church in Memphis, Tennessee. The *Journey Points with Jesus* Series offers short conversations about practical issues that allow for us to 'live close with God' and to 'live out God's Will' in the world. CCG believes the primary mission of the Church is to proclaim the Good News of Jesus Christ and to equip God's people with the tools needed for full maturity in faith in Jesus. Therefore, we believe once a person comes to know and confess Jesus Christ as their Lord, Savior and Friend, our primary responsibility is to live life in such a way as to witness to God's love and grace so that others (our friends, relatives and, even, the strangers along our path) will be transformed in Christ. *Journey Points with Jesus* are the markers of faith along our everyday journey that allow us to draw close to Jesus and help others to do the same. This particular book begins with the 'marker of prayer' and its incredible importance for developing the full measure of our relationship with God through Jesus Christ.

At the end of this short book is a section entitled "New Beginnings". If you do not know Jesus Christ as your Lord and Savior or if it has been a long time or a far distance from when you last proclaimed Him as so, take time to read through this final section. Carefully read the questions. Reflect on the answers. Don't put this book down until the small quiet voice in your soul really 'gets your attention'.

Finally, the staff of Jericho Springs and members of Christ Church simply want to remind you that you are valuable and loved. God has gone to great effort to bring you into relationship with Him. It is never too late to call out for help or to begin again. Our Congregational Care ministry at Christ Church is available to pray with you and discuss your next steps. If not already a part of the family, we would love for you to be a part of Christ Church. We love you. But, more importantly, we hope you know how much God loves you.

Be Salt and Light, my friend... You Matter!

Shane Stanford
Lead Pastor
Christ UMC

INTRODUCTION
'AN HONEST ASSESSMENT'

Prayer is one of the most important interactions in all of humanity. Prayer, as defined by both Scripture and many secular works, is a 'core discipline' of most any expression of spirituality. Every major religion includes prayer (or some form of meditation) as part of the spiritual journey or routine. And, for most religions, prayer serves as a major connection between the adherent and the religion's deity/spiritual authority.

But, for Christians, prayer is more than a 'discipline' or 'journey'. Recently, I finished a study of the prayer life of Jesus of Nazareth as described in the Scriptures of the books, Matthew, Mark, Luke, John and Acts. There are over 60 times in Scripture when Jesus would go away to pray, meditate, pray for a particular circumstance or situation, or respond to the need of a brother or sister. For Jesus, prayer was at the center of his relationship with the Father God, and he organized and lived his life as such.

Before you begin this short focus on your prayer life, I want to ask you some rather direct questions. I don't ask them to press you or cause you any discomfort. Quite the contrary... I believe so much in the power of what you are about to read and commit yourself to doing that I want you to be fully AND honestly prepared to make the trip.

As mentioned above, I wrote a book entitled, 'What the Prayers of Jesus Tell Us About the Heart of God'. When I wrote the book, I had been in ministry for over 20 years. I had written 10 books before that one. I thought I knew the most important principles about prayer. I WAS WRONG!

I am not the same person after spending time with Jesus while he spent time in prayer. My heart for communicating with the God of Universe is different, more aware of what a privilege and honor it is for me to be in God's presence AND then to have a chance to 'ask of him anything'.

Thirty years ago, I contracted HIV and Hepatitis C through blood transfusions used to treat my hemophilia—a condition that keeps a person from clotting or healing correctly. The only treatments for many years were those transfusions of human blood. Thus, over 90% of my generation of hemophiliacs died from AIDS due to the transfusions. Since then, I have dealt with serious complications and other medical issues—from open-heart surgery, diabetes, loss of my eyesight in one eye, etc. It has not been an easy journey. But, I learned from an early age the importance of prayer, and I can say honestly that prayer has sustained me throughout my life.

And, yet, with all I thought I knew about prayer, learning how Jesus prayed not only re-engaged my prayer life, it changed it. I realized that prayer was not static or just a powerful experience when or if we really decided to put our minds to it. No, it is dynamic and organic in nature, springing up from the deepest places in our lives, reminding us that God is always present whether we realize it or not.

That is what I want you to consider before you begin this conversation. Are you prepared for a dynamic experience of prayer, not just a religious rite that you use from time to time (or maybe even daily)? And, do you truly want prayer to be something that exists 'between' you and God or that allows God to live IN you? These are important questions, and they sit at the heart of what it means to truly 'be how you pray'—instead of just communicating.

The following are some questions I asked myself as I began my time 'away' with Jesus during his prayer life. These questions formed not only my approach to the moment, but even more important, framed how the residual power of prayer affected the whole of my life from that moment on. They became important for the health of my spiritual journey, and I believe they will be just as important for you.

Take your time with these questions and faithfully respond to them. I believe it will make an incredible difference in your journey.

1. Have you chosen a journal, and are you prepared to make your entries every day? No process for prayer is more important than being able to 'look back' and see how God is answering and responding to your prayers.

2. Do you have a time/place/routine that allows for you to pray uninterrupted with your focus on Christ? Prayer is not a static event, but you will need to begin the process with the ability to put your complete focus on God so that you can learn how prayer shapes and molds your conversations with him. One of the biggest mistakes I made in my previous prayer life was spending a great deal of time 'talking' but making no provision for 'listening'.

3. Make sure you have your Bible available and present during your prayer time. Most people pray with a devotional guide or a notebook but without their Bible present. Even if you don't plan to use it, the Bible is the 'Word of God' and is still the primary means for God to speak back to us. Why would we want to move God's Word

to the side when 'conversation' is the very experience we are wanting with him.

4. Chose an accountability partner in this process—someone who can hold you 'in check' as you pray and go through the process of being in God's presence. I am not asking you to pray with anyone but to have someone who will hold you accountable for your presence in prayer with Christ.

5. Finally, and this will sound a bit unusual, but worship will be of huge importance during this journey. I have found over the last few months, that my worship both informs and serves as an outlet for my time with Christ. Prayer experienced in such close connection with Christ fills you in ways most of us are not prepared. We need the ability to respond, share our emotions, raise our hearts and lives in what we are hearing, saying, feeling. THAT is what worship is all about. Find a time and place of worship that allows for you to not only be in God's presence but to celebrate the presence of God throughout the whole of your life.

As I have said, I want nothing more than for you to be knocked off your feet by the power of what prayer can do in your life. I can't wait to hear how these moments with God affect both the religious and, yet also, the normal everyday experiences of your life. Again, this is more than the discipline of prayer—you are spending time with Jesus—your friend, Lord, and Savior. Get ready.

PART ONE
'AT A LOSS FOR WORDS'

Ms. Edna was the best piano teacher in the tri-County area. No one would have dared say otherwise, even if it had not been the truth. But, it was the truth and everyone who had shared the keys with Ms. Edna knew it.

She was a strict disciplinarian, though. Her students worked harder than other students of other teachers. "You must give yourself to the art of piano", Ms. Edna would say. "No exceptional pianist practiced unexceptionally!"

The art of piano. That is always what Ms. Edna saw in her craft. Teaching piano was not just music or technique; it was part of the classics of the human condition, like painting and poetry. Ms. Edna believed to play the piano was to offer the world a gift, and how should one give a gift but with joy and anticipation. As many of her students stated at Ms. Edna's retirement party, the world was given something very precious each time the notes made their way through the air.

But, as so often happens, time catches us when we least expect it. Ms. Edna developed significant problems with arthritis and was, finally, unable to teach or play the piano well. To protect her hands, she gave up both.

Yet, after several years of not playing, Ms. Edna knew something was missing in her soul. She couldn't play as well as in years before, and she certainly could not play for extended stretches. But, it wasn't her hands that needed the music; it was her soul.

Ms. Edna also loved the Lord. She had grown up in church, and had, her whole life, played for her local congregation. When she retired from piano, the choir at the local church where she played stopped calling, and her music wasn't the only part of her life that went quiet.

That is when Ms. Edna started praying about the next "notes" in her life. The answer was a bit unusual. She noticed in the local paper advertising from a couple who were getting married and needed a guest pianist for the ceremony. She was excited to play at the wedding. But, while at the wedding, the grandfather of the bride mentioned that his wife was a "shut-in", unable to attend church any longer. Ms. Edna asked if she could contact his wife and play for her over the phone. He readily agreed, and the afternoon after the wedding, Ms. Edna spent one solid hour playing the "favorites" of the woman via telephone. And, this gave Ms. Edna an idea.

She had read a story in her local newspaper about a "phone-a-prayer" service in the community. People could call the number listed and submit a prayer request. It had been moderately successful, and Ms. Edna wondered if the same could work for piano playing.

She prayed for clarity, and when she received it, she put an ad in the same local newspaper offering to play a hymn favorite for those who called the listed telephone number. Ms. Edna projected to a friend that she thought maybe 25 people would call during the first week—based on what had happened with the "phone-a-prayer". Twenty-five was a good estimate… for the first hour. Within the first two hours, nearly 75 people had called. And, by the end of the four hours of the first afternoon of her new project, Ms. Edna fielded over 200 hundred requests. Within two weeks of the ad in the newspaper, Ms. Edna was forced to ask for volunteer administrative help. By the end of the first month, there were "fill-in" pianists to make sure no one was missed.

To say that Ms. Edna's idea was a success would be quite the understatement. But, what was most revealing about her project was that, when people were asked about the interaction with Ms. Edna, few of them mentioned the quality of her piano playing. No, the biggest "hit" was Ms. Edna herself. Not only did many of the callers make future requests on a regular basis, they told their friends about it. Her heart, spirit and sweet nature was the most beautiful music, and those "notes' reverberated deep within the souls of those who called.

Ms. Edna did more than play wonderful music; she became the music and people loved it.

Most of my prayers take one of two forms. I am either asking God to help with some problem or situation, or *I am thanking God* for helping with some problem or situation. And, to make matters worse, I am usually bargaining with God in the second form as to how I will *thank Him more* if he *blesses me more*. It is a horrible cycle, but one that has dominated my prayer life and, in many ways, symbolizes how I connect to God at times. You know what I mean-- we will talk to God when we need Him or when we are in trouble. But, Jesus describes prayer in a much different frame.

Matthew 6 is at the heart of the Sermon on the Mount. In the previous chapter, Jesus has taught the Beatitudes as His list of ministry values, and then encouraged the disciples to be "salt and light" to the world. But, as He transitions into the meat of the sermon, one of the first topics he confronts is prayer.

Jesus doesn't simply discuss prayer in the traditional, ritualistic form. No, prayer, as described by Jesus, is both a process and, more importantly, the by-product of a relationship. In fact, Jesus would argue that you couldn't have one without the other. And, the implications are two-fold. First, prayer is a marker for how our relationship with God unfolds. Quite frankly, whether we know it or not, we see ourselves in our prayers, and our prayers mirror the state of our souls. But, second, our prayers also are seen in us. How we pray becomes the framework for how our faith "hits the ground". Thus, like my grandfather liked to say, in both our relationship and our ritual of faith, "we are how we pray"- and that is where the name for this book was born.

Several years ago, I took my daughters to the concert of a contemporary Christian artist. By the end of the night, the concert had turned more into a worship service. My family does not come from an expressive background in worship. Growing up, if someone raised their hand in my local church, folks thought you had a question. It was not progressive for praise and worship to say the least. The same was also true for my wife's background.

Of course, that did not mean we did not worship or feel God's presence. And, we had "loosened up" in the years since our childhoods. But, we had not experienced the freedom to move through the facades of our heritage as much as I believe The Holy Spirit intended. And yet, at this concert, my entire family felt something from the time we entered the auditorium. We loved the music of the artist we had come to hear, certainly, but there was something else—something that spoke to each of us in very different, personal ways.

So, toward the end of the concert, as the artist moved the congregation to a point strictly focused on God's presence and praise of Him, I looked over to see my eldest daughter raising one of her hands toward Heaven. There was a look on her face of utter joy and peace. She sang and swayed to the music, holding her hand high. It was a beautiful sight. However, within just a few moments of this amazing gesture of worship for her, I then watched as she slowly lifted her other hand. For those next moments, my little girl looked like an angel gathered around the throne. There were so many emotions running through me. I was a father deeply moved by the expressions of authenticity and depth of my daughter's spirituality. I was a humbled child of God. I was an engaged worshipper. But, more than anything, standing there watching my daughter worship, I was envious. I was envious of such abandon in the presence of the Creator of the Universe. Yes, with all of the feelings at that moment, most of all I wanted what my daughter had found.

Driving home from the concert, my eldest daughter and I took a moment to talk about the evening. She was glowing, and I could tell that she was both holding tightly to what she was experiencing but also wanting to shout about it at the same time.

"Honey, I saw you worship tonight. You looked so peaceful. May I ask what you were feeling?" I said.

"Daddy," she readily answered, "It was amazing." Her smile was huge by this point. "I was standing there and God was telling me to raise my hand. I know it sounds crazy but I could hear him, Daddy."

"I believe you, sweetie" I said. "I hear Him from time to time, too."

"So, I raised my hand. And, I just stood there. But, it wasn't enough." She said.

"What do you mean, Darling?" I asked.

"God kept talking to me. Then, finally He said 'It is okay, Sarai Grace, you can raise the other hand, too.'"

As my daughter stood there describing what her conversation with God meant to her, I understood. I understood the depth of what talking to God means. But, even more, I also understood what listening to what He tells us transforms inside of us. It does more than raise our hands; it raises our potential and our possibilities in His grace. My daughter did more that night than worship with hands raised; she raised her heart and became available to where God would lead next. No matter if it is a concert turned worship, or the simple prayer of a child, even God's whispers shout loud if we are willing to listen.

I love the first words of Mercy Me's song, *Word of God* speak. *I'm finding myself at a loss for words, and the funny thing is,*

11

its okay. The last thing I need is to be heard, but to hear what you would say...

Reflection:

1. What is God saying to you during your current prayer life and experience?

2. What would deepen your ability to respond to God's call in your life—*like Ms Edna?*

3. Are you holding back in your response to God's call to worship him? Why? How could you open your heart (and hands) more to his pleading?

It is okay, my child... you can raise the other hand, too.

PART TWO
'THE LORD'S PRAYER
FOR GOD'S PEOPLE'

Scripture Text: Matthew 6: 9-13

9 Pray like this: Our Father who is in heaven, uphold the holiness of your name. 10 Bring in your kingdom so that your will is done on earth as it's done in heaven. 11 Give us the bread we need for today. 12 Forgive us for the ways we have wronged you, just as we also forgive those who have wronged us. 13 And don't lead us into temptation, but rescue us from the evil one. (Common English Bible-Abingdon Press)

For many years, I sat in worship in various churches within my faith tradition and heard the pastoral prayer followed by a recitation of the Lord's Prayer. It did not matter if the church was large or small, new or older, suburban or urban; the process was always the same—a liturgist or pastor would say the prayer, the congregation would follow, and when finished, the worship moved on. Many times, it was as though the entire congregation was on autopilot, kept numb by the repetition. I often wondered if Jesus intended this kind of response the first time he prayed the Lord's Prayer. Somewhere deep inside, I doubted it.

In the Gospels, prayer for Jesus was always a personal, powerful and profound experience. He pushed against the rote prayers of the priests; he warned the disciples to spend time praying in order to fight demonic possession, and he, personally, retreated time and again to spend 'conversation time' with the Father. To Jesus, prayer was never a static moment of ritual within a worship service. It was never simply the "next" part of a discussion with God or God's people. No, prayer for Jesus was deeper, more personal, filled with untapped possibilities in the presence of God. And, more than anything, He wanted His followers to embrace it—no; He wanted them to become *it*.

Therefore, when the Disciples asked Him to teach them to pray, he responded with a prayer that seemed more "outline" than a ritual that would be repeated for centuries. In fact, that is what I believe the Lord's Prayer was—an outline that provided the scaffolding for not only how we are to pray, but also why we pray what we do. If one reads closely, as though through the lens of a teacher answering the question of his students, The Lord's Prayer is less liturgy than lesson plan. After having treated the Lord's Prayer as repetitive litany for two thousand years, it may seem strange to consider the Lord's Prayer any other way. However, why would Jesus, a teacher bent on moving people into personal, useable relationships with God, add another facet to the very ritualistic bonds from which He sought to release us? The answer is that he wouldn't. No, the purpose of the Lord's Prayer was to outline for us the beginning of the conversation with God, not to be the only way to experience prayer.

Seeing the Lord's Prayer from this framework, we learn amazing lessons from Jesus about not only our prayer life but also the process of intimate communication with the Creator. Thus, the outline is the key itself to what Jesus taught his disciples, not so much to be repeated word for word but principle to principle, focus point to focus point.

Lets take a look at how Jesus not only intended for the Lord's Prayer to shape the way we talk with God, but also the way God talks with us and how we live the Good News everyday. If *I am how I pray*, these are our *personality traits* according to Jesus.

1. *Praise-- Verse 9- Pray like this: Our Father who is in heaven, uphold the holiness of your name.*

The Lord's Prayer begins with Praise, not from a corporate perspective but praise and worship understood, as one would enter Holy ground and into a sacred presence. There is a sense of awe and wonder when we find ourselves in such places, an *other worldliness* that speaks to something different and bigger than us.

We understand this as human beings. Certainly, when we travel to Holy places such as the Holy Land, the Vatican, or other markers of our faith, we feel something different than our normal routine. We should. That is what the *otherness* is all about. But, we don't have to go to *Holy* places to have this feeling. We are wired up to pause in places and spaces that mean bigger things than usual. For instance, I remember the first time I visited The White House, I stood so long in the East Room that my group had to come back and get me to move along.

I stood in the East Room remembering all of the incredible meetings that had taken place there— weddings, press conferences, and the resignation of a President. The most important part is that the space held the moment and they were special. A friend of mine recently was invited to the Oval Office. He is a very knowledgeable, accomplished man. But, when he walked into the Oval Office, he said he actually went a bit weak in the knees. It is no secret that the Oval Office was designed to impress foreign dignitaries and to give the President a "home field advantage". However, the most important quality is that at this spot in this place, not just a man sits as President, but the vestment of power for the free world rests.

We should not be the same when we arrive in the Oval Office. And, even more profound, Jesus said we should not be the same every time we confront and meet the Father in prayer. The first part of the Lord's Prayer is an *ushering into* the Holy Presence of a Holy God. That alone deserves our praise!

2. *Holy Humility— Verse 10- Bring in your kingdom so that your will is done on earth as it's done in heaven.*

The next part of our conversation with God always leads from Praise of God to a clear understanding of Who God is and, in return, who we are. The supplication of God's will to be done among us as it is in Heaven is not an accidental image. In Jesus' day, it was difficult to distinguish between God's will and the will of the religious leaders. The culture had become so interwoven into the face of religion that even the most beautiful parts of God were distorted beyond recognition. By asking for God's will to come alive in us as powerfully as the Will of God is expressed in Heaven… well… think about how that would look.

Several years ago, at the church I serve as pastor, we had the privilege of hosting two dayschools. The first was created 53 years ago and has been a foundation of religious education in our community for decades. The second (Cornerstone Prep) was, at the time, a small, missional school that specifically reached into the most under resourced parts of our city. The students from both came from precious families, and they were a joy to watch. But, their paths were very different in so many critical ways. To be a part of a congregation who had the responsibility FOR BOTH to love them, care for them, teach them, and, yes, pray for them, still means the world in so many ways.

One day during the school session, while walking around our facility, I stopped in the courtyard to see the students of Cornerstone Prep playing "red rover". It is an old, children's game whereby two lines form. The challenge from one line is to send over a member of the other line. Once the person is "named" to go, he or she takes off running as fast as they can toward the other line. The folks in the line to which the person is running join hands and hold as tightly as possible. If the person running toward the line is able to bust through the tightly gripped hands, he or she is able to take one of the members of the line back with him or her to his or her original line. If not, well, then he or she must stay.

On this particular day, Cedric was called to "come on over…" Cedric took off running toward the line; however, before he got to the line, he slowed, and, then, eventually, stopped all together. He had noticed that the little girl he was running toward (we learned later) looked "scared". So, he stopped. It was an amazing scene. In a world where we are taught to "win at all costs", the lesson of Heaven played out in the courtyard of Christ Church.

I have seen these examples time and again in the little lives of these children. It reminds me of Jesus' own words saying, "Unless you come unto me as a little child…" Our best lessons are learned by drawing close to the impressions of Heaven in our very mortal places. As we appreciate those moments and places in front of us, we find ourselves ever closer to God. There is a reason we pray that God will transform earth into His place again. We need it. And, somewhere deep inside, we know it.

3. *The Basics— Verse 11- Give us the bread we need for today…*

Though we are encouraged to not make our prayers about us, it does not mean that God does not want to hear our concerns and requests. In fact, this section of the Lord's Prayer meets us at our most personal place. *Our daily bread* is not just about food or what our body needs, but all of those requests that keep us healthy and whole in Christ.

There is a story told of orphans after World War II who were discovered living in a bombed out shelter in an abandoned concentration camp. A group of Catholic nuns had been charged with taking care of their needs and nursing them back to health. However, each night, though they had been provided every basic need the nuns could think of, the children would weep and cry themselves to sleep. The wailing was muted most of the night but heard nonetheless.

The nuns thought of every option for helping the children to sleep through the night, to find some peace in their wrecked, battered little lives. However, nothing seemed to help, until one of the older nuns, who had been praying through the situation, went into the local village and bought loaves of bread from the village baker. She brought the loaves of bread back to the orphanage and, before bedtime, gave each child a loaf of bread. That night the nuns tucked in their children, loaves of bread within their arms. And, the nuns wondered if this night would be different. It was.

The night was silent. No weeping. No crying. The next morning the nuns arrived to sleeping children, each holding tightly to their loaf of bread. Their needs, *their daily bread*, was not just a list of bread, water, and supplies. Their basic need went deeper, and God met it through the hearts and service of those nuns. Much was filled that night as their tears stopped, and little of it had to do with their stomachs. The same could be said for our own hunger. God knows our needs. But, more than praying them so that God can hear those needs from us (God is already fully aware of our needs), God encourages us to name our basic needs so that we hear them as well. Too often our basic needs stand between us and who God is crafting us to be. By naming them, we realize that God is aware and prepared to make sense of them—are we ready to let him?

4. Starting Over, Everyday— Verse 12- Forgive us

for the ways we have wronged you, just as we also forgive those who have wronged us.

I have always been passionate about exercise. Okay, that is not accurate. Okay, maybe that was a downright lie. Truth is that I exercise, but I have never really liked it. In fact, I would rather be doing just about anything else at any point in the day. And, yet, I know how important it is for me to exercise in some way each day.

The same is true for this part of the Lord's Prayer. Most people (me included) like to think of this part of the prayer as "for special occasions". This is only needed for the really big transgressions. In fact, when I teach on this section of the Lord's Prayer, many comment on having thought of this as related to particular debts or situations. But, that is not the focus of Jesus' teaching in this section of the Lord's Prayer. Jesus meant debts in the present imperative tense, meaning that the *debts* are the everyday ways that we miss God's truth, not just by dishonesty, but by living a lie as well. And, if it was not enough that we have to come clean on our own transgressions, we are called (and expected) to forgive others as well.

I remember the first house we purchased. It was in a new neighborhood that had not had the proper surveys done for the sale of the lots. As you can imagine, this was a very serious issue. But, for our lot, the most important problem was where our neighbor's fence would sit. When we found out that our boundaries were not good, we asked him to wait before he put up his fence, knowing that if the survey was, indeed, off, we would have to adjust a lot of work. Unfortunately, our neighbor (who was more than a little difficult) proceeded without the surveys. And, sure enough, his fence was almost a foot on our property. We finally resolved the issue, but we learned a couple of lessons in the process.

First, boundaries are very important. We need them, not to keep people out, but to make sure our own identity can thrive and be safe enough to exist in the midst of others. But, second, we learned to always take time to "survey" the surroundings. Many times, life is not as it may seem and it takes a little extra work to make the path straight, the way safe, and the fence… well, accurate.

Our trespasses are only as devastating as they are maliciously unaddressed. Our prayers remind us that nothing substitutes for taking the time to be in relationship and to care how that relationship is growing healthier. This part of Jesus' prayer was not about wasting time on the rights and wrongs of life (as is so often interpreted) but focusing on the reason why those *rights and wrongs, mistakes and broken hearts* have such long-term effects.

This part of the prayer receives the most 'naming' in my journals. Since our journals should be private and personal, I usually name the persons or situations specifically, with which I need assistance. I encourage you to be specific, too. These are real people and situations. God knows exactly whom you are naming, but too often we are the ones who shy away from facing the confrontation 'head on'. To not do so leaves too much unsolved and the Adversary with far too much power. Set those boundaries first by naming them and then move faithfully and reasonably down the path together.

5. *Meeting the Bad Things With the Best Things— Verse 13- and don't lead us into temptation, but rescue us from the evil one.*

Today, nearly two-thirds of all marriages will end in divorce. When asked, 75% of men said they would have an affair with someone to which they are not married if they knew they wouldn't get caught. Before you get upset at all men, 68% of women said the same thing.

We live in a world where bad things happen. And, we live in a world where people do bad things. But, Jesus' prayer pushes at the belief that we don't have to be overwhelmed, uninformed or unprepared by those two truths. Yes, we face a host of sins that define and distract us. We are tempted, and we confront evil on a regular basis. But, this part of the Lord's Prayer says clearly that the God of the Universe believes enough in you and me to stand in the gap of those temptations and to protect us from that evil.

This part of the prayer reminds me that God confronts the bad things in our lives with better things. What are those things? Simply, they are spending time with Him and then living in the world as though *you have spent time with Him.* It really is that straightforward. Most of us underestimate the importance of proximity when it comes to fighting the weakest parts of our spiritual constitutions. But, nothing substitutes for being in the presence of God.

When my middle daughter was five years old, a kid bullied her in her class. We did not know the full extent of the problem until we went to a Sunday school class party and the family of the little girl who had been bullying our daughter was there. We noticed that our daughter, who is always the life of the party, stayed very close to us-- her mom and dad. When we asked her about it later, she replied that the little girl had been "picking on her". Where did our daughter run? To her parents. We were her safe place.

The same is true for our relationship with God. Sometimes, the world bullies us. It often pushes us around. The Adversary wants nothing more than to destroy us, but he will be satisfied with simply distracting us enough to debilitate us in our faithfulness. But, like children, when it all gets to be too much, we draw close to God. We run to the Father. He is our safe place.

But, what if we didn't have to be in that place. What if we could face our nightmares and struggles long before they haunt us and taunt us? That is Jesus' prayer. The God who is God of Heaven and earth, who is strong and certain, whose standing at the center of our needs—that God will stand around the corner for us, too, waiting in the shadows well ahead of where we have to go. Run to him. You don't have to be afraid.

The Lord's Prayer is an outline to a prayerful life. It is also a diagram for a dedicated life. Jesus wants us to do more than spend our thirty minutes in a good devotional time (which is important). No, He wants our prayers to become the blueprint for who we claim to be, and for whom others claim they see when we are around.

My friend, John, is a praying man. In fact, all of his life, prayer resonated as more than words but as the doorway to his relationship with God. He told of learning to pray from his grandmother, a wonderful, mighty saint who prayed like "her life depended on it". But, her prayers did not stop simply as words hanging in the air. She always told John that "our prayers mean little if we aren't courageous enough to live them". John never forgot those words.

My friend left his small northern Arkansas hometown not long after high school. He attended the University of Tennessee and then earned a law degree from Yale University. He was a "good church going boy", John described of himself, and he always remembered to say his prayers, just as his grandmother taught him. His journey took him first to Atlanta and then to Memphis. His life was filled with success, family, and all the accomplishments a smart, southern boy could imagine

When he retired from practicing law, he settled into his Memphis home, volunteered at local ministry shelters and at his church. He took over the day-to-day operations of the old family business, and he enjoyed the life he had worked so hard to establish. All the while, he prayed daily, and, as he liked to say, "tried to live as faithful to life, as life had been to him". From most accounts, it was a journey well lived.

But, John felt as though something was missing.

Sure, he had tried to live a "good life" and to remain faithful to all of the lessons those who loved him at taught him from his young age. And, yet, as he grew older, he felt as though God wanted something more from him.

Enrolling in a prayer ministry class at his local church, John began praying the Lord's Prayer from a much different angle and focus than he had at any time before in his life. The prayer class taught him to pause and truly soak in what it meant to be in the presence of the Creator of the Universe, what "daily bread" meant—for those who had it and for those who didn't-- , and what it meant to truly be delivered from the evil of this world. The result was a conversation started deep inside of John's soul that he could not shake.

He talked with his pastor and several trusted friends about the stirrings in his soul. Each of them offered great advice, but John knew the real answers were not so much in a plan or process, but in the personal ways God wanted to meet John through his prayers. John began spending more focused time with God, not so much praying or talking, but listening. He was amazed at what you could hear God say to your soul when you stopped long enough to really take it all in. The words were fresh, powerful and, at times, critical of places John had missed as the "hands and feet of Jesus".

These prayer moments with God became journaling and study opportunities; eventually leading to various other ways throughout the days and weeks that John sought God's guidance and wisdom. The more John spent time with God, the more his decisions, thoughts, values and impressions of the world around him changed. He stopped seeing the world through the veil of his own wants and desires, and actually began to see the world through the eyes of Christ. Most of what he saw engaged him, and brought him a sense of inner wholeness. But, other parts of what he saw in a world broken from God's original intentions tore at John's heart. The closer he drew to God, the more he saw what God saw and, in places, it troubled him.

One area John saw the world differently was in hunger and poverty among the most vulnerable on the planet. In particular, John became concerned with the needs of orphans starving in sub-Saharan Africa. As difficult as the situation and circumstances were in many areas, equally disturbing was the simplicity at which these issues could be addressed but weren't. The reasons were many and played from the all too familiar song sheet of corruption, cultural distinctions, and prejudice. But, the answers remained fairly attainable, though the questions themselves caused many, at times, to be uncomfortable.

John was a fan of Norman Borlaug. Dr. Borlaug invented a first version of dwarf wheat—wheat that could grow and develop but would not fall over and become susceptible to insects and drought. In fact, Dr. Borlaug was credited with saving over 1 billion lives with this discovery. John loved the simple description of one stalk of wheat, previously unusable in so many parts of the world, now available for mass distribution to those in need.

During the time John prayed for God's guidance as to what he was supposed to do with the rumblings in his spirit, Normal Borlaug passed away. Attending the memorial service for Dr. Borlaug, John met a group that specialized in providing usable bags of wheat and other food sources to starving areas of the world. Unlike other distribution methods, these one family bags only needed water, and a family instantly had porridge like substance that provided the nutrients people needed to survive. John prayed about how God could use him to distribute these bags of wheat.

Arriving back at his church, John set up the first of several "packing days" whereby members could help fill the family food bags, label them for distribution and then pack them in crates for the hardest hit areas of the world.

Not knowing how many would attend the first of these "packing days", John prepared to construct, at most, 30,000 bags of wheat—a noble gesture for a first time ministry.

By the end of the first week, over 400,000 bags of wheat had been developed and prepared for shipping. And, as the first season of "packing days" finished, nearly 2 million bags were constructed. What began as the simple prayers of a man looking for God's next steps became a regimen of hope that would change and save lives half way around the world.

Today, John's small ministry venture has grown into a successful mission project that not only feeds the hungry stomachs of folks in countries around the world, but, for the families working to put the bags together, it offers spiritual nourishment for hungry souls across the street. How did this happen? One could say it was the ingenuity of a brilliant man listening to the lives of other brilliant men and women following the example of another brilliant man. Follow that? And, yes, it is true that the cause of grace and hope often unfold one life, introduction, and intersection at a time.

But, before all of that, as important as those moments were, I believe the help millions of people received through John's efforts and leaderships started at the knee of his grandmother reminding him that his prayers matter. My friend, John, with all that he became in this world, was first and foremost *how he prayed.*

PART THREE
'I AM HOW I PRAY'

My first church was very small. In fact, we joked that if you were under 60, you were in the youth ministry. We had around 45 people who worshipped with us on a regular basis. The vast majority of them (95%) were over 65. They were an incredible group of saints who loved the Lord, who served faithfully, and prayed diligently.

One particular woman, who I will call Pat, invited my wife and me to her house on a regular basis. She was a wonderful cook, and she loved having the preacher over for lunch, dinner or for dessert.

On a visit to her home I discovered a beautiful painting of a little girl kneeling and praying in a field of daisies. The little girl had her hands clasped, eyes closed, and wore the sweetest smile. As I looked closely to the picture, I noticed that there was a gentle tear coming down the edge of her cheek. It was subtle, not seen except to the person who took time to study it.

I stood there looking at the painting, wondering what was going on in that little girl's life. With such a sweet smile in such a wonderful setting, what would cause her to cry? Were they tears of joy? Was there something we could not see? Certainly, but what?

I walked back into the dining room where my hostess was preparing another of her wonderful dishes to serve. "You were looking at the painting again," she said.

"Yes" I answered. "It is just so beautiful."

She could tell that I was considering something I had seen.

"You want to know about the tear?" She replied.

I was shocked at her insight. But, I knew that anyone who had spent enough time with the painting would be interested in this small yet powerful detail.

"Yes," I said. "It seems so subtle and yet it screams at you the longer you look at it."

"The little girl in the painting came from a broken family." My friend answered. "She was the apple of her father's eye until he found another family to love more. He left her mother and her sisters and moved a thousand miles away." I stood amazed, knowing there had been more to the story.

"What happened to her. Was that why she was crying?" I replied.

"Sort of" my friend said. "After her mother and father divorced, she would go into the field next to her house. It was full of daisies. She liked to kneel and pray. She talked to God on a regular basis. When her father left her, she found a new Father to take His place."

"And the tear?" I asked.

"The tear was when she realized that this Father would never leave. He would never abandon her."

"How do you know all of this?" I inquired.

"Well," my friend said softly. "I'm that little girl."

I had not known my friend's story. She went on to tell me of how her father had made attempts to re-connect to her, but how he would eventually let her down one time after another. He was a good man, but not a good father. And, by the end of his life, he lived in the shadow of much regret, and, most importantly, without his daughters.

Through it all, my friend learned to pray. She didn't pray because it was the right thing to do, or because it was part of her daily devotional. No, she prayed in the field of daisies and late at night and in the deepest most personal places, because it was where she met the One who would never let her down. Her prayers became a testament to what real relationship in faith could be. Her prayers became the language of her life.

My friend was a wonderful person of faith. She loved the Lord. And, she knew the difference of what saying she loved God and actually clinging to him for survival meant. For every daisy she picked and prayed over, God embraced her little heart, dried her tears, and painted a picture that never grew old. But, she DID grow older, and her life took many twists and turns. And, yet, in so many ways she was still that little girl kneeling in the field. No matter how many years passed, like all of us, she WAS how she prayed.

PART FOUR
'PRAYING AS I AM… OR AT LEAST HOW I SHOULD BE'

I developed the following seven questions for my personal prayer time with God. I share them with you only as a means of framing what you have read and for modeling the personal effect and journey I believe prayer should be. I developed these questions (and the subsequent 'sub-questions') as a means to 'center' my life on those aspects that engage my prayer life—beginning where I was and then growing forward.

1. How does your prayer life reflect your relationship with God?

Note: Communication is an important part of any relationship. How would you rate the health of your relationship with God based on the quality of your prayer time together.

2. What do you pray for on a daily basis?

Note: Journaling the topics and issues for which we pray is not just important in the moment but for looking back to see both our pattern for the needs we consider important AND for measuring how God answers/responds to those needs.

3. How does your prayer life resemble your daily walk?

Note: Make a list of with two columns. In one column list the issues or needs you prayed for today. In the other column, list the issues or tasks that you addressed during the day. At the bottom, analyze whether the two lists resemble each other. If so, how? If no, why?

4. What causes your prayer life to become too self focused?

Notes: In the same list as before, make a star by every prayer request that is about you personally. Then highlight or underline the others. How does this list look? Is it overwhelmed with highlighted or underlined areas? Or do the 'stars' win out? These last two questions may seem overly simple, but one will be surprised at how such exercises show us the imbalance in our daily prayer routine.

5. How do those moments and intersections in your prayer life affect your overall relationship with God?

Notes: Take a moment to look at what you have listed as your prayer requests. Ask this question... if your requests were answered as you have prayed them, how would your relationship with God look? With others? We are often surprised by how our prayer requests 'land' when answered in the 'everyday world'.

6. How does the outline of the Lord's Prayer impact your prayer life?

Notes: This question reminded me each day of the importance of prayer to God. By following Jesus' command to "pray like this", we see both the intimate nature of prayer for our relationship with God and the discipline required to pray at such depth on our spiritual journey.

7. What does an "answered prayer" look like?

Notes: This is not a trick question. Most people have never fully reflected on this question simply because their prayer requests are either too simple or too vague. But, ask yourself the question. If you can't either see the answer in relation to the question itself or you cannot imagine how God might respond, then your prayer request needs refinement or refocusing.

Ok. You have spent a great deal of time 'thinking about prayer'. Now, lets actually pray. I have written the following prayer for you. It is based on a prayer I prayed for myself during my days of spending time with Jesus and his prayer life. The words are not random or without meaning for the journey you are now on. I hope you feel that as you pray.

Prayer: Gracious God, we thank you for the privilege of prayer. You give us the opportunity to be in your presence, to talk to you whenever we need, and with the promise that you are listening. What can we say that you have not already heard? And, yet, you listen anyway. You love us when we are selfish, and you love us when we are broken. But, Father, help us to know that you never leave. And, because of that, we bring not only our requests and concerns but also all that we are to you. We want to be known by you, and to know you completely. We want to become so close to you, that we become what we pray. We love you, Father. In Jesus, Amen.

PART FIVE
"PRAYING LIKE JESUS"

A WEEKLY GUIDE FOR THE BIBLICAL
FRAMEWORK FOR CHRIST'S PRAYERS

As we have mentioned, many of us pray, but do we pray like Jesus. I guess I will keep asking that question until I get to heaven. I don't ask it out of some spiritual grandstanding but sincerely, knowing that the time I spent with Jesus as He spent time with the Father changed me. I truly do not want anyone to miss the chance to be affected as I was by the simple presence of the Godhead (all three in one) spending time deeply involved in this most simple of spiritual practices among the most holy and complex of theological settings. The thought still gives me goose bumps.

The following is a weekly guide for praying like Jesus. It is rather simple, as Jesus' prayer time with the Father tended to be. And, it has one primary focus—communication with the Creator of the Universe who deeply wants to communicate with you and me.

Now, I have had my critics who have said that distilling the prayer experience between Jesus and the Father to something so simple and personal reduces the Sovereignty of God. Well, I will let the theologians debate the full measure of that argument. All I can offer is this... what is more sovereign than One who gives his subjects the opportunity to be present with them and to express their nature, thoughts, concerns, dreams, etc. in equal measure.

The One offering such a connection is not depleting their sovereignty, they are simply raising the beauty and nature of our humanity—which by the way, the Sovereign One created in the first place. So, to me, though I will never fully understand the nature and power of God (or God's sovereignty), I DO trust Him. And, He has made himself known and available to us. I will not miss that chance.

Here is your suggested, weekly prayer guide.

Sunday: Sabbath (with worship and prayer in your worship community)

Monday: Pray for God's Wisdom—so often we are left with only earthly knowledge of right and wrong. This is important but it does not meet the needs of understanding the world (and our place in it) with the 'other worldly wisdom' of God. God doesn't want you to rely simply on what you know—he wants to provide real wisdom that still changes the world.

Tuesday: Pray for a Heart that Praises God—our lives become so distracted by the things of this world that we often sacrifice purpose for 'just getting by'. God wants us to focus our hearts and lives on him so that we begin and end our day with real meaning. God will fill in the parts between how he begin and end that day, and you can be assured that it will mean something more.

Wednesday: Pray for Unity in the Body of Christ—Jesus prayed for unity to the Father more than any other topic. Jesus saw what disunity could do to people and their lives. We are called to be God's children and God does not want God's children fighting or at odds. There is too much to accomplish in and through Jesus.

Thursday: Pray for a New and Faithful Relationship with God—we are not meant to remain 'aliens or strangers' (as the Apostle Paul states) but to take our full place and rights as children of a king. God has given us the best of himself in Jesus and this is the start of a new and wonderful relationship with God. But, so often we settle for old rags and dingy settings to call home. We are loved more than that... we are valuable because of what God has done for us through Jesus. Now, live like it.

Friday: Pray the Lords' Prayer-- Use the Guideline suggested in this book—The Lord's Prayer is more than an outline but a set of holy markers for praying as Christ has taught us. The outline in this book provides a detailed way to pray like Jesus in the prayer that bears his name.

Saturday: Journal Your Prayer Life for the Week and spend time in specific Intercession for the Needs of Others—journaling is a form of praying. We learn this through the prophets. But, like anything, if it is not taken seriously, it will lose its potency. Use this day to journal and be in conversation with God. Conversation, by the way, means mostly listening. Get out God's Word, reflect on your prayer life during the week, and hear what God has been trying and still tries to tell you.

PART SIX
ARE YOU LOOKING FOR A NEW START IN LIFE?

Hello Friend: I have taken some privilege in expecting most who are reading this book are already followers of Jesus Christ. But, people find their way into these types of conversations through a variety of means. And, there is no 'one route' that God uses to 'draw God's people close to himself'. So, no matter how you have arrived at this conversation... welcome.

But, before I let you go, I wanted to make sure that you had the chance to make your new walk with Christ 'real'.

The following is entitled 'A New Start in Life'. We created this set of questions and responses as a means to challenge people to accept Christ as their Lord and Savior and then to 'begin again'. Again, as we have said many times, prayer is more than a spiritual ritual, it is about relationship—particularly your relationship with Jesus Christ. No matter what you have learned or discussed over the last few pages, none of it matters unless Christ sits at the center of both you and your journey.

Follow the steps below to begin your journey close to the heart of God. Don't be afraid-- God has been waiting for you.

You're not here by accident. God loves you. He

wants you to have a personal relationship with Him through Jesus, His Son. There is just one thing that separates you from God. That one thing is sin.

The Bible describes sin in many ways. Most simply, sin is our failure to measure up to God's holiness and His righteous standards. We sin by things we do, choices we make, attitudes we show, and thoughts we entertain. We also sin when we fail to do right things. The Bible affirms our own experience – "there is none righteous, not even one." No matter how good we try to be, none of us does right things all the time.

People tend to divide themselves into groups - good people and bad people. But God says that every person who has ever lived is a sinner, and that any sin separates us from God. No matter how we might classify ourselves, this includes you and me. We are all sinners.

- *"For all have sinned and come short of the glory of God." Romans 3:23*

Many people are confused about the way to God. Some think they will be punished or rewarded according to how good they are. Some think they should make things right in their lives before they try to come to God. Others find it hard to understand how Jesus could love them when other people don't seem to. But I have great news for you! God DOES love you! More than you can ever imagine! And there's nothing you can do to make Him stop! Yes, our sins demand punishment - the punishment of death and separation from God. But, because of His great love, God sent His only Son Jesus to die for our sins.

- *"God demonstrates His own love for us in this: While we were still sinners, Christ died for us." Romans 5:8*

For you to come to God you have to get rid of your sin problem. But, in our own strength, not one of us can do this! You can't make yourself right with God by being a better person. Only God can rescue us from our sins. He is willing to do this not because of anything you can offer Him, but JUST BECAUSE HE LOVES YOU!

- *"He saved us, not because of righteous things we had done, but because of His mercy." Titus 3:5*

It's God's grace that allows you to come to Him - not your efforts to "clean up your life" or work your way to Heaven. You can't earn it. It's a free gift.

- *"For it is by grace you have been saved, through faith - and this not from yourselves, it is the gift of God - not by works, so that no one can boast." Ephesians 2:8-9*

For you to come to God, the penalty for your sin must be paid. God's gift to you is His son, Jesus, who paid the debt for you when He died on the Cross.

- *"For the wages of sin is death, but the gift of God is eternal life in Jesus Christ our Lord." Romans 6:23*

Jesus paid the price for your sin and mine by giving His life on a cross at a place called Calvary, just outside of the city walls of Jerusalem in ancient Israel. God brought Jesus back from the dead. He provided the way for you to have a personal relationship with Him through Jesus. When we realize how deeply our sin grieves the heart of God and how desperately we need a Savior, we are ready to receive God's offer of salvation. To admit we are sinners means turning away from our sin and selfishness and turning to follow Jesus. The Bible word for this is "repentance" - to change our thinking about how grievous sin is, so our thinking is in line with God's.

All that's left for you to do is to accept the gift that Jesus is holding out for you right now.

- *"If you confess with your mouth, "Jesus is Lord," and believe in your heart that God raised him from the dead, you will be saved. For it is with your heart that you believe and are justified, and it is with your mouth that you confess and are saved." Romans 10:9-10*

God says that if you believe in His son, Jesus, you can live forever with Him in glory.

- *"For God so loved the world that He gave his one and only Son, that whoever believes in him shall not perish, but have eternal life." John 3:16*

Are you ready to accept the gift of eternal life that Jesus is offering you right now? Let's review what this commitment involves:

1. I acknowledge I am a sinner in need of a Savior - this is to repent or turn away from sin

2. I believe in my heart that God raised Jesus from the dead - this is to trust that Jesus paid the full penalty for my sins

3. I confess Jesus as my Lord and my God - this is to surrender control of my life to Jesus

4. Receive Jesus as my Savior forever - this is to accept that God has done for me and in me what He promised

If it is your sincere desire to receive Jesus into your heart as your personal Lord and Savior, then talk to God from your heart:

Here's a Suggested Prayer:

> *"Lord Jesus, I know that I am a sinner and I do not deserve eternal life. But, I believe You died and rose from the grave to make me a new creation and to prepare me to dwell in your presence forever. Jesus, come into my life, take control of my life, forgive my sins and save me. I am now placing my trust in You alone for my salvation and I accept your free gift of eternal life."*

If you have made this decision to follow Christ as your Lord and Savior, please let us know.

Click here to send us a message. We want to pray for you and celebrate this important first step in Christ.

However, we also want to encourage you to find a community of believers to share with on this journey. You are not meant to make this journey alone.

ABOUT JERICHO SPRINGS

The 'Journey with Jesus Series' is a partnership between Christ Church, Memphis and Jericho Springs Resources, LLC. This series seeks to meet people at the intersections of life and our deepest spiritual questions. Both of these organizations play an important role in my own spiritual journey. Christ Church is not only the congregation I pastor but they are my family. I love my walk with them. Jericho Springs Resources is an organization my wife and I created to develop resources that matter to our family and we hope matters to you and yours as well. The following is a brief description of these important places in my personal life.

Jericho Springs Resources, LLC

The mission of Jericho Springs Resources, LLC is the development of media outreach resources that proclaim the Good News of Jesus Christ and equip the Body of Christ for full maturity in following the example and life of Jesus.

Values:

1. We believe that Jesus Christ is the Son of God and the hope of the world.
2. We believe that following the example of Christ

transforms the individual heart and life so that families, friendships, churches and communities are changed forever and for good.

3. We believe that the Body of Christ engages the issues and challenges of this world by offering new ways of viewing the potential of grace, forgiveness, and boldness of the Gospel

4. We believe that Christian resources should convene a series of conversations, both personal and corporate, that provide new directions and maturity in Christ.

5. We believe that to love Jesus must also include loving like Jesus for the Good News to be complete.

ABOUT THE AUTHOR

Dr. Shane Stanford is:

- The Senior Pastor of Christ Church in Memphis, TN.

- Adjunct Instructor of Practical Theology at Asbury Theological Seminary.

- President/CEO and Founder of Jericho Springs Resources.

- Co-Host (with Dr. Maxie Dunnam) of 'We Believe in Memphis' TV Program

- Teacher and Executive Producer of 'You Matter' Media Outreach Ministry—including the StudyCast Learning Curriculum

A former church planter, Shane is the author of 15 books as well as numerous articles and curricula. He is the co-host of Abingdon Press' Covenant Bible Study, used now in over 1,000 churches nationwide.

Shane is a graduate of the University of Southern Mississippi (B.A. *cum laude)* and Duke University (M.Div.). In 2014, Asbury Theological Seminary awarded Shane a doctorate (D.D.) for his years of *faithful and innovative ministry.*

Along with Dr. Maxie Dunnam, Shane has been responsible for the creation and development of several important ministry endeavors over the past several years in Memphis—including the founding of Asbury-Memphis at Christ Church and the Mosaic Program for Mental Health Care for the Under-resourced.

Shane is married to his high-school sweetheart, Dr. Pokey Stanford, and they are the parents of three daughters, Sarai Grace (18), Juli Anna (15), and Emma Leigh (11). The Stanfords live in Germantown, TN.

For information about Dr. Stanford, go to:

www.makinglifematter.org
Making Life Matter Ministries

www.cumcmemphis.org
Christ Church, Memphis

18846472R00032

Made in the USA
Middletown, DE
25 March 2015